T0190847

Little People, BIG DREAMS™

# MARY KOM

Written by
Maria Isabel Sánchez Vegara

Illustrated by
Jen Khatun

Frances Lincoln
Children's Books

In the heart of Manipur, in northeast India, lived a girl named Mangte Chungneijang who later became known as Mary. She grew up fishing, chopping wood, taking care of her siblings, and helping her parents in the fields.

Mary loved running and playing all kinds of sports.
At school, she was a great athlete.

But no matter how well she ran, some students wouldn't take her talent seriously.

One day, she heard about a young man from a nearby village who won a gold medal boxing at the Asian Games. His name was Dingko Singh, and he became her inspiration. From that day on, Mary dreamed of becoming a boxer too.

TEA STaLL
Coffee
Juice
Herbal

Of course, to become a champion, Mary had to start from the bottom. It took courage to even find an academy where she could begin training.

Still, once she put the gloves on,
she felt she was born to be in the ring!

In just two weeks, she learned the basic punches: jab, cross, hook, and uppercut. With each move, Mary gained strength, speed, and confidence. Soon she was winning fight after fight.

But for a while she kept her achievements to herself.

Her parents thought boxing was a man's sport and might ruin Mary's chances of finding a husband.

When they saw in the paper that she had won the state championship, they couldn't believe their eyes!

It took Mary three long years to get her parents to accept that a girl could box.

After that, she not only relied on her hard work but on the support of her entire family. By the age of nineteen, she was a world champion!

Some time later, Mary met a young man named Onler. He became her husband and her biggest fan. After they had twins, Mary decided to take a break from boxing.

Some said her career was over. But when she felt ready, she worked hard to come back stronger than ever.

Women's boxing made its debut at the London 2012 Olympic Games, and Mary was the only female boxer to represent India.

Despite fighting against bigger and heavier opponents,
she still managed to win a bronze medal.

Back home, India's president honored Mary's achievements by nominating her to the Rajya Sabha—part of the country's government.

She also became an animal-rights activist,
using her voice to fight for every living creature.

She made history as the only woman to win six world boxing titles, earning her the nickname "Magnificent Mary."

After twenty years in the ring, Mary had become a legend and one of India's most decorated athletes.

In Manipur, Mary set up a boxing school. She wanted to ensure that a new generation of female boxers could follow in her footsteps.

There, she also offered free training to kids from families who couldn't afford it.

And little Mary, the girl who reached for the stars with her boxing gloves, will forever be an inspiration to young athletes.

She proves that courage can turn
dreams into victories.

# MARY KOM

(Born 1983)

2006

2013

Mangte Chungneijang Mary Kom was born in Kangathei village in the state of Manipur, northeast India. Her parents were farm workers and earned little money, so Mary helped out by doing chores and caring for her siblings. At school, she enjoyed playing sports and took part in volleyball, track and field, and soccer. In 1998, when she was fifteen, boxer Dingko Singh won a gold medal at the Asian Games. He was also from Manipur and inspired many people from the state to take up the sport—including Mary. Two years later, she won her first gold medal at the state championships. Some people, including her parents, thought that boxing was just for boys, but Mary soon proved them wrong. Her career in the ring took off, and by 2010, she had won five world amateur

2018

2024

boxing championships. During this time, she also got married, became a mother, and started a boxing foundation. In 2012, she made her Olympic debut and won a bronze medal, beating heavier opponents with her quick footwork and precise moves. Her sporting achievements meant that, in 2016, she was nominated by the president of India to be a member of the Rajya Sabha—the upper house of the country's parliament. There, Mary took part in debates about causes close to her heart, like encouraging women in sports. While a member of parliament, she made history by winning her sixth world boxing championship—the first woman to do so. Mary's story reminds us that by believing in ourselves we can achieve our dreams and help others to do the same.

Want to find out more?

Have a read of these great books:

*Women in Sport: 50 Fearless Athletes who Played to Win* by Rachel Ignotofsky

*Stories for South Asian Supergirls* by Raj Kaur Khaira


Original idea of the series by Maria Isabel Sánchez Vegara, published by Alba Editorial, s.l.u.
"Little People, BIG DREAMS" and "Pequeña & Grande" are trademarks of
Alba Editorial s.l.u. and/or Beautifool Couple S.L.
First published in the US in 2024 by Frances Lincoln Children's Books, an imprint of The Quarto Group.
Quarto Boston North Shore, 100 Cummings Center, Suite 265D, Beverly, MA 01915, USA
Tel: +1 978-282-9590 **www.Quarto.com**

A CIP record for this book is available from the Library of Congress.
ISBN 978-0-7112-9810-1
Set in Futura BT.

Published by Peter Marley · Designed by Sasha Moxon
Commissioned by Lucy Menzies · Edited by Molly Mead
Production by Robin Boothroyd · Sensitivity evaluation by Guntaas Kaur Chugh
Manufactured in Guangdong, China CC072024
1 3 5 7 9 8 6 4 2

Photographic acknowledgements (pages 28-29, from left to right): 1. New Delhi, INDIA: Indian boxer MC Mary Kom (C) is watched by silver medalist Steluta Duta (L) of Romania and bronze medalist Jong OK (R) of North Korea as she celebrates during prize ceremony, after winning a gold medal, 23 November 2006 © MANPREET ROMANA/AFP/Stringer via Getty Images. 2. Nagaland, India. 24th Oct, 2013. Indian women Boxing Champion and Olympic Medalist, MC Mary Kom shows some moves to school children after inaugurating the Niathu Sports Festival at Dimapur, India's northeastern state of Nagaland © ZUMA Press, Inc./Alamy Live News via Alamy Stock Photo 3. Mary Kom is an Olympic boxer from the eastern Indian state, Manipur. She is the only woman from India to become World Amateur Boxing Champion for a record six times © Sondeep Shankar via Alamy Stock Photo. 4. 7th Jan, 2024. MUMBAI, INDIA: Masterclass on boxing & self defense by Legendary Indian boxer Mary Kom. (Photo by Satish Bate/Hindustan Times/Sipa USA) © Sipa US/Alamy Live News via Alamy Stock Photo.

# Collect the *Little People*, **BIG DREAMS**™ series:

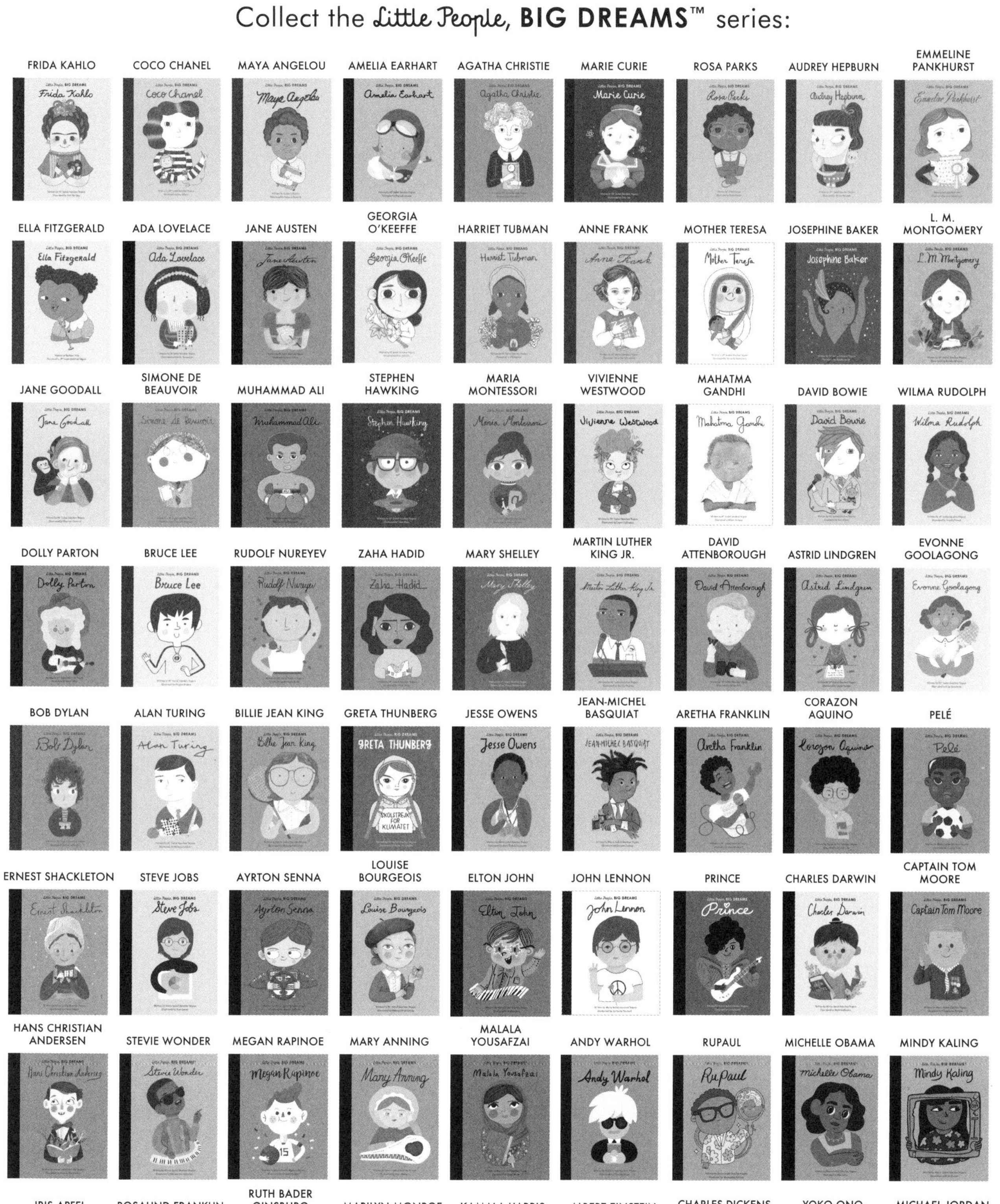

FRIDA KAHLO · COCO CHANEL · MAYA ANGELOU · AMELIA EARHART · AGATHA CHRISTIE · MARIE CURIE · ROSA PARKS · AUDREY HEPBURN · EMMELINE PANKHURST

ELLA FITZGERALD · ADA LOVELACE · JANE AUSTEN · GEORGIA O'KEEFFE · HARRIET TUBMAN · ANNE FRANK · MOTHER TERESA · JOSEPHINE BAKER · L. M. MONTGOMERY

JANE GOODALL · SIMONE DE BEAUVOIR · MUHAMMAD ALI · STEPHEN HAWKING · MARIA MONTESSORI · VIVIENNE WESTWOOD · MAHATMA GANDHI · DAVID BOWIE · WILMA RUDOLPH

DOLLY PARTON · BRUCE LEE · RUDOLF NUREYEV · ZAHA HADID · MARY SHELLEY · MARTIN LUTHER KING JR. · DAVID ATTENBOROUGH · ASTRID LINDGREN · EVONNE GOOLAGONG

BOB DYLAN · ALAN TURING · BILLIE JEAN KING · GRETA THUNBERG · JESSE OWENS · JEAN-MICHEL BASQUIAT · ARETHA FRANKLIN · CORAZON AQUINO · PELÉ

ERNEST SHACKLETON · STEVE JOBS · AYRTON SENNA · LOUISE BOURGEOIS · ELTON JOHN · JOHN LENNON · PRINCE · CHARLES DARWIN · CAPTAIN TOM MOORE

HANS CHRISTIAN ANDERSEN · STEVIE WONDER · MEGAN RAPINOE · MARY ANNING · MALALA YOUSAFZAI · ANDY WARHOL · RUPAUL · MICHELLE OBAMA · MINDY KALING

IRIS APFEL · ROSALIND FRANKLIN · RUTH BADER GINSBURG · MARILYN MONROE · KAMALA HARRIS · ALBERT EINSTEIN · CHARLES DICKENS · YOKO ONO · MICHAEL JORDAN

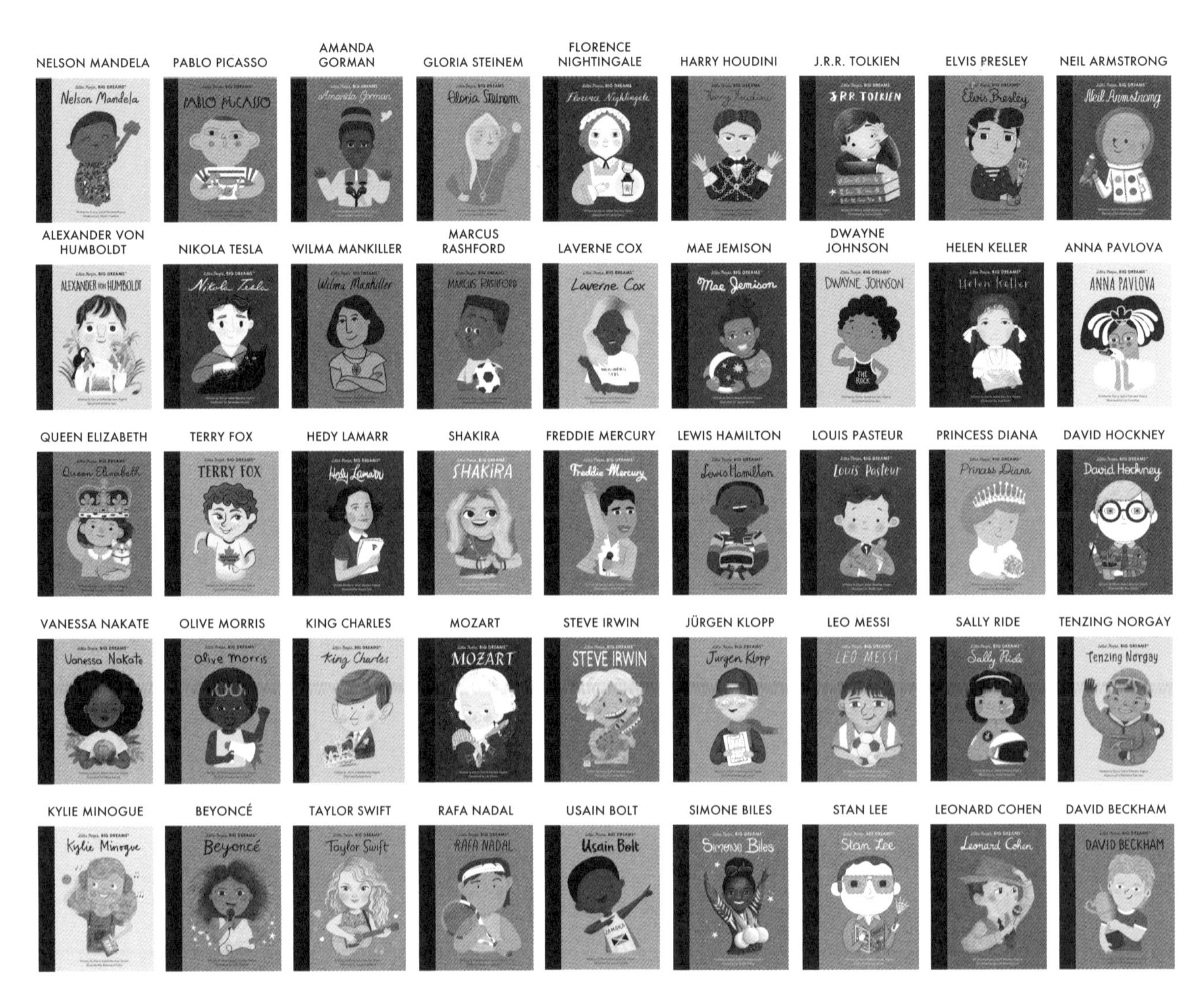

Scan the QR code for free activity sheets, teachers' notes and more information about the series at www.littlepeoplebigdreams.com